ROBIN HANLEY

VILLAGES IN ROMAN BRITAIN

Second edition

SHIRE ARCHAEOLOGY

2

For Jenny

(Top) Reconstruction of a typical Romano-British village
(see figure 1). (Drawing by Sarah Lucy)
(Bottom) Aerial photograph of the settlement at Milton, Cambridgeshire
(see figure 4). (Photograph and copyright: Ben Robinson, 1994)

British Library Cataloguing in Publication Data:
Hanley, Robin
Villages in Roman Britain. – 2nd ed. – (Shire archaeology; 49)
1. Villages – Great Britain – History
2. Great Britain – Antiquities, Roman
I. Title 936.1'009734
ISBN 0 7478 0411 7

Published in 2000 by
SHIRE PUBLICATIONS LTD
Cromwell House, Church Street, Princes Risborough,
Buckinghamshire HP27 9AA, UK.
(Website: www.shirebooks.co.uk)

Series Editor: James Dyer.

Number 49 in the Shire Archaeology series.

ISBN 0 7478 0411 7

First published 1987; second edition, with new text and illustrations, 2000.

Printed in Great Britain by
CIT Printing Services Ltd, Press Buildings,
Merlins Bridge, Haverfordwest, Pembrokeshire SA61 1XF.

Contents

Acknowledgements

I am grateful to the following for their assistance: James Dyer (series editor), Jeffrey May, Andrew Poulter and Colin Pendleton for advice on the text for the first edition; Sarah Lucy for the specially commissioned village reconstruction drawing; Bernard Rawes for photographs and advice relating to his excavations in Gloucestershire; Dr Tim Potter of the British Museum for permission to reproduce photographs and the excellent reconstruction drawing from his superb report on excavations at Stonea Grange. Simon Palmer of the Oxfordshire Unit was most helpful in the provision of photographs and plans of the unit's work at Claydon Pike. Many thanks to Ben Robinson of Peterborough City Council for permission to use his excellent aerial photographs of Cambridgeshire sites and Tim Malim of the Cambridgeshire County Council Archaeological Field Unit for photographs of work at Throckenholt. Derrick Riley was very helpful concerning aerial photographs of Dunstan's Clump. Permission for use of other photographs and illustrations was kindly provided by the following: Richard Kent, B. Cunliffe, A. Detsicas, the Royal Commission on Historical Monuments (England), R. Leech, W. Wedlake, G. Jobey, Chelmsford Archaeological Trust, the Somerset Archaeological Society and P. Fowler. David Wilson of the Committee for Aerial Photography at Cambridge was very helpful with the selection of images.

List of illustrations

1
Introduction

The sites that are the subject of this book are those Romano-British rural settlements falling between the categories of individual farm and major town.

The systematic study of the settlement pattern within the Romano-British countryside – with the notable exception of villa sites – has been comparatively neglected until recent years. Well into the 1970s the research interests of most archaeologists studying the Roman period tended to focus on the more immediately rewarding sites of villas, towns and military installations. Even after a dramatic increase in the level of interest in Roman rural studies during the last twenty-five years of the twentieth century, only a small number of the sites discussed in this book have been adequately investigated.

It now seems likely that population levels in Roman Britain – estimated at between four and six million – may be usefully compared with those of the medieval period. Such levels of population would require a degree of rural organisation much greater than previously supposed as it must be assumed that only a minority of people would have lived within the major towns of the province. All the evidence suggests that village-type settlements fulfilled a vital role within the highly populated Romano-British countryside.

Before any discussion of the main forms of rural settlement encountered in the landscape can take place, it is necessary to consider the rather baffling range of terms used by archaeologists to describe such sites.

2
Describing village-type settlements

The terminology available to anyone studying those Romano-British rural settlements falling between the categories of the individual farmstead or villa and the towns of chartered (*colonia* or *municipium*) or tribal (*civitas*) capital status is both varied and fraught with difficulties. The danger of anachronism is ever present, with even the term 'village' having close associations with the medieval period.

A brief glance through a selection of recent archaeological publications illustrates some of the problems encountered in attempting to describe village-type settlements in a uniform way. The bewildering array of terms currently used by Roman archaeologists includes 'village', 'small town', *'vicus'*, 'larger rural settlement', 'lower order settlement', 'lowest-order market centre', 'non-villa settlement', 'native settlement', 'roadside settlement', 'local centre', 'local market centre', 'proto-urban centre', 'hamlet' and 'nucleated settlement'. The most commonly used of these terms tend to be 'village', 'small town' and *'vicus'*.

1. Reconstruction of how a typical Romano-British village may have appeared. Buildings of different function are set inside individual plots, alongside a road. Both agricultural and industrial activity is taking place within the settlement. (Drawing by Sarah Lucy)

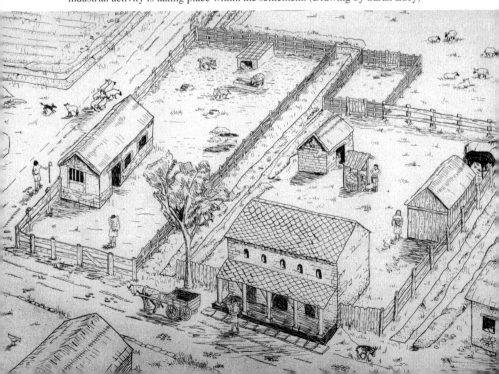

Village

R. G. Collingwood, the great archaeological authority on Roman Britain, used the term 'village' as long ago as the 1930s to describe poorer sites of essentially native (i.e. Iron Age) form, producing limited evidence for any degree of Romanisation. Enclosed sites of distinctive prehistoric form, such as Woodcuts in Dorset, were thought to represent typical examples of such village settlements. Collingwood considered that truly Romanised sites were characterised by such site forms as the villa, town and fort. In the late 1950s A. L. F. Rivet argued that the term 'village' should be removed altogether from the vocabulary of the Romano-British countryside, suggesting instead that the 'native' farm and Romanised villa represented the only units of rural settlement at this time.

An alternative view was presented by Sylvia Hallam in the 1960s, following the identification of many complexes of village-type settlements and linked compounds around the Wash in south Lincolnshire. Hallam adopted a range of descriptive terms, including 'small hamlets' (consisting of two to three farms), 'large hamlets' (four to six farms) and 'small villages' (seven or more farms). She also made the important point that archaeologists studying the Roman landscape should expect to find both individual and grouped ('nucleated') settlements.

In recent years many Romano-British scholars have adopted the term 'village', and it is frequently found in the context of other provinces in the Roman Empire. A useful definition of the term might be as a rural population centre of variable size, falling between the categories of single farm holding and town, a site serving as a centre for agricultural and industrial production and distribution. The term is probably best used as a generalisation rather than as a specific category with a long list of attendant criteria.

Small town

An increasing number of larger rural settlements have been gathered together under the rather vague term of 'small town'. These sites are clearly not towns in the Roman legal sense, being of neither *colonia, municipium* or tribal (*civitas*) capital status. Such major towns are characterised by a range of standard features, including a planned layout of streets and a common range of public buildings and amenities.

The lack of agreed criteria associated with the use of the term 'small town' has resulted in a vast cross-section of sites being rather unsatisfactorily grouped together, with defended and highly urbanised – yet essentially unplanned – sites like Water Newton, near Peterborough, and Godmanchester in Cambridgeshire at one end of the spectrum, and open village-type settlements like Kingscote in Gloucestershire and Camerton in Somerset at the other. Settlement size appears to have been of little relevance in determining either relative importance or economic activity (see chapter 9).

Small towns were described as a distinct Romano-British settlement form by Malcolm Todd in 1970, although he was the first to warn that they should not be viewed as a uniform group. More recently, Richard Hingley has suggested that the term 'local centre' might be more appropriately applied to these sites, correctly stressing the important economic role these settlements played in the life of the province.

Clearly, no one term will ever be completely satisfactory because of the impossible requirement of grouping such a diverse range of settlement types under one neat heading. For example, some recent lists of Romano-British small towns include only those sites where there is evidence of a defensive circuit, thereby excluding many significant settlements.

Vicus

This is a Roman legal term that was probably applied to many of the larger settlements that were not of *colonia, municipium* or tribal (*civitas*) capital status. It is clear, however, that during the later Roman period the strict legal definition of the term became significantly loosened.

The *vicus* may be viewed as the lowest unit in the hierarchy of the province's tribally based administrative system, holding limited powers delegated by the local *civitas* capital or chartered town of the administrative territory in which the settlement lay. Essentially, when used in the context of the Roman countryside, the term can be used to describe even very large settlements which lack municipal authority, although in the later Roman period sites such as Water Newton (*Durobrivae*) in Cambridgeshire and Ilchester (*Lindinis*) in Somerset may have been elevated to the legal status of town, a trend identified elsewhere in the Roman empire.

It is likely that, throughout the Roman provinces, most *vici* were not independent settlements in administrative terms, coming under the jurisdiction instead of the nearest official town or military station, although there is evidence from other provinces for some *vici* having their own independent councils and administrative arrangements. As far as settlements are concerned, there is a lack of historical evidence for their being contemporarily described as *vici*, although for fort sites on the northern frontier this status is made clear by inscriptions. Here the inhabitants are recorded as *vicani*. Finds from the sprawling settlement at Water Newton (*Durobrivae*) include a *mortarium* stamp describing the *vico Dorobrivis*.

The difficulty in using the term *vicus* has been noted by writers such as Peter Salway, who stated that this flexible term can apply to a village-type settlement, a fort-side settlement, a district of a town and even part of a legion. The confusion that could be caused because of the specific legal meaning of the term – particularly in the later Roman period – means that its use should be strictly limited to discussions of site function rather than site form.

Conclusions

Despite the many qualifications applicable to the use of each of these terms, it is still helpful to have access to them in the sort of general discussion presented in this book. It would appear that the terms 'village' and 'small town' present the fewest difficulties, although the 'local centre' suggested by Richard Hingley remains quite appealing, stressing as it does the vital economic role performed by these settlements.

In summary, the term 'village' can probably be used to describe any type of settlement falling between the single farming unit and major town. 'Small town' indicates a site which, by its activities or extent, transcends the norms of rural settlement life and includes a combination of the following elements: a specialised industrial activity; a suggested administrative significance; positioning on an important roadway; a high level of economic activity including industrial production; possession of a market or fair function; extensive settlement size and evidence of internal organisation.

3
Preserved landscapes

The intensive use of the land and the emergence of complex farming landscapes across much of the lowland zone are developments that can be recognised during both the Iron Age and Roman periods. The preserved landscapes such as those identified on the upper Thames at Lechlade and Fairford (Gloucestershire) are best seen from the air (figure 2). Recorded remains include drainage ditches, buildings, attached enclosures, linked droveways and field systems. Subsequent excavations carried out on part of this site complex at Claydon Pike (figures 19–22) revealed a sizable settlement with an organised street plan and evidence for the presence of both stone and timber houses.

This landscape is comparable to other parts of the province, where intensive aerial photography and fieldwork have revealed much about

2. A Romano-British rural landscape preserved as cropmarks in the modern fields of Lechlade and Fairford parishes, Gloucestershire. (Photograph: University of Cambridge copyright reserved)

3. Aerial photograph of the settlement at Bullocks Haste, Cambridgeshire. Note the dramatic contrast in the quality of the site remains between the pasture and ploughed fields. (Photograph and copyright: Ben Robinson 1996)

4. Aerial photograph of the extensive settlement at Milton, Cambridgeshire, showing the complex pattern of plots and enclosures. (Photograph and copyright: Ben Robinson 1994)

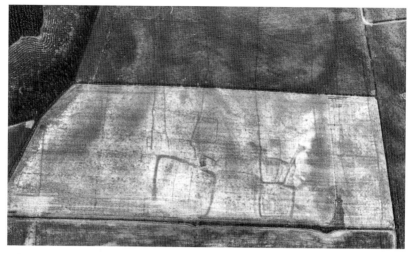

5. Cropmarks of the site at Dunstan's Clump, Nottinghamshire. (Photograph: D. Riley)

the organisation of the countryside. For example, complex farming landscapes have been identified in the Cambridgeshire Fens at the well-preserved sites at Bullocks Haste and Milton, near Cambridge (figures 3 and 4). Comparable detailed survey work has also been carried out in Nottinghamshire, again resulting in targeted excavations (figure 5).

Such programmes of intensive survey and selective excavation are potentially of great value to the study of Roman rural archaeology in that they are able to place settlement sites within the context of a wider farming landscape. This is also the case with regional studies, which are necessary if the density and form of Roman rural settlements within any given area are to be fully appreciated.

4
Iron Age to Roman Britain

Upland Britain contains very well-preserved evidence for clustered village-type communities of houses dating from the later prehistoric period onwards. Extensive complexes of 'hut circles' – the remains of circular stone-built houses often associated with other structures, including stock enclosures – are a relatively common feature within the upland landscapes in areas such as Bodmin Moor in Cornwall, Wales and much of Scotland's Highland region (figure 6). Sometimes these farms lie in isolation, but there are many instances where buildings cluster together into what may be described as village-type communities.

In the lowland zone there is evidence for the existence of substantial Iron Age communities within hillforts such as Crickley Hill (Gloucestershire) and Maiden Castle (Dorset). Large, open village-type settlements have also been identified at many locations including Dragonby (Lincolnshire) and Langwood near Chatteris (Cambridgeshire). At Langwood the excavators suggested that this open settlement contained about one hundred individual buildings, possibly acting as a regional centre for the Iceni tribe. On a number of sites there is clear evidence for settlement continuity from the Iron Age into the Roman period, although in the case of both Dragonby and Langwood the Roman settlement appears to have been at a reduced level.

Dragonby represents a useful example of a large and prosperous Iron Age settlement with evidence of trading links into continental Europe. During the Iron Age the site consisted of a number of circular timber huts associated with rectangular enclosures. In the Roman period these

6. Well-preserved prehistoric stone hut circles on Bodmin Moor, Cornwall.

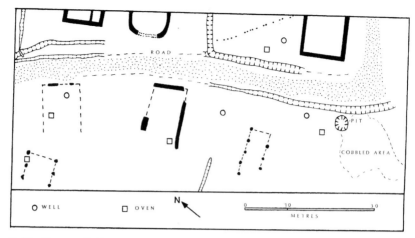

7. The Romano-British phase at Dragonby, Lincolnshire. Buildings of stone and timber construction are set inside ditched enclosures beside the main road through the settlement. (After May)

structures were replaced by characteristically Romanised rectangular stone buildings aligned end-on to a metalled road and set back within individual ditched enclosures (figure 7).

The well-known 'nucleated' village at Chysauster (figure 8) in south Cornwall provides another good example of continuity from the prehistoric period, with the main phase of site occupation commencing in the first century BC and continuing into the second century AD.

8. The well-preserved village at Chysauster, Cornwall. (Photograph: University of Cambridge copyright reserved)

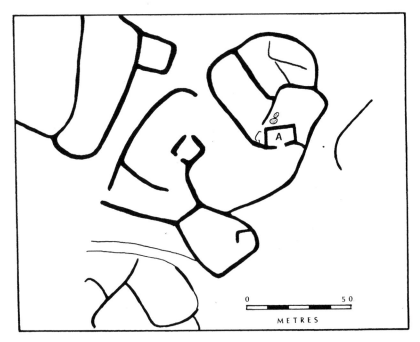

9. The site at Butcombe, Somerset. 'A' is the only excavated building. (After Fowler)

It can be argued that the study of village-type settlements in Iron Age Britain has been as neglected as that in the Roman period. In this context it is worth remembering that until the late 1930s it was believed that many Iron Age people inhabited 'pit dwellings'. It was not until 1938 that the existence of the lowland Iron Age settlements of the type familiar today was established following excavations at Little Woodbury (Wiltshire) by Bersu, the German archaeologist. He demonstrated that 'pit dwellings' were in fact storage pits and that Iron Age people inhabited well-made timber roundhouses. A similar village site has been excavated at Gussage All Saints (Dorset), dated by pottery finds to the period between the fourth century BC and the first century AD.

The typical building form in the lowlands during the Iron Age period was the circular timber hut constructed from either a single or a double post ring. Several examples of these buildings have been reconstructed at the Butser Ancient Farm in Hampshire. This form was widely replaced during the Roman period by rectangular buildings, which became the norm in the centuries following the conquest of Britain. Rectangular Iron Age buildings are recorded, however, including examples from within the hillfort site at Crickley Hill.

A number of village sites, including Dragonby in Lincolnshire and

Braughing and Baldock in Hertfordshire, produce evidence for settlement
continuity from the Iron Age into the Roman period. As will be seen in
the next chapter, such continuity is particularly apparent on those sites
in upland areas, although examples are also recorded from the lowland
zone, as at Butcombe in Somerset (figure 9) and Chalton in Hampshire.
Of about 140 village sites identified by the author in a study area
incorporating most of Somerset and Gloucestershire, some thirty-six
sites provided clear evidence of Iron Age activity, with it being suspected
at many more.

It is likely that the vast majority of the Romano-British rural population
was derived from existing Iron Age communities, and there is no
evidence of a large influx of new peoples, despite the changes that took
place in settlement form and political power. The population of the
prehistoric and Romano-British countryside probably remained largely
static.

The discovery of Iron Age material in association with evidence of a
Roman settlement does not always imply direct continuity and the
evidence for each individual site requires careful consideration. A useful
example is provided by the substantial Roman settlement at Stonea in
the Cambridgeshire Fens (figures 28 and 29). Excavations by the British
Museum revealed evidence of a thriving and prosperous Iron Age
settlement associated with the nearby defended enclosure at Stonea
Camp. However, the site appears to have been largely abandoned during
the early Roman period, possibly in the aftermath of Icenian tribal
uprisings against Rome in either AD 47 or 60–1. The important Roman
settlement at Stonea Grange, centred on an imposing stone tower, was
created later, between AD 130 and 150, indicating a possible settlement
gap of a generation.

5
Villages in upland areas

In the upland areas of England and Wales the Roman conquest was to have only a limited effect on local native communities that were already organised into village-based societies. The economy of the villages in these regions was primarily pastoral and exhibited many more Iron Age traits than Roman.

The limited impact of recognisably Romanised settlement forms in the upland zones of areas such as Wales, Cornwall and much of northern England is clear from the lack of villas and towns. It is also apparent in the absence of village settlement characteristics that are encountered elsewhere in the province, such as building construction methods, site layout and the quality of associated finds.

Within upland areas such as the northern Pennines the absence of the traits of Romanisation encountered so frequently in the lowland zone may be attributed to a number of different factors: poorer marginal land directly resulting in limited disposable income; a lack of the external investment apparent in more challenging lowland areas (such as the Fens); a lack of the marketing potential offered by towns and villas in other parts of the province; the effects of a protracted military presence in the form of frontier or fort garrisons, with many upland sites lying within militarised zones. A certain hostility to Roman ways in some of the remoter tribal areas is also likely to have been a major reason why the forces of Romanisation made little headway.

The cultural isolation apparent in the poorer quality of archaeological finds from these sites resulted in many Iron Age village settlements continuing into the Roman period largely in their prehistoric form, with the timber or stone-built circular hut being the most common building type. A well-known example of such continuity is provided at Chysauster in Cornwall (figure 8), although many other areas provide instances of continuity in settlement form.

The only truly Romanised villages in the upland zone tend to be the isolated fort-side settlements recorded in a number of areas; the best examples are the well-preserved sites on Hadrian's Wall at Housesteads and Chesterholm (*Vindolanda*), described as *vici* on inscriptions (figure 10). Away from the forts, some settlements around Hadrian's Wall probably exhibit a limited degree of Romanisation in the form of rectangular buildings.

The most Romanised of settlement types, the villa and the town, are largely absent from these upland areas, as was the marketing potential they offered to native rural communities. It appears that the local native

10. The fort and *vicus* at Chesterholm (*Vindolanda*) on Hadrian's Wall. (Photograph: University of Cambridge copyright reserved)

aristocracy was either too poor or too proud to build villas, and investment from outside does not appear to have been forthcoming. In the north the few villas to be found are all located south of Hadrian's Wall, outside the extensive zone of military control from which villa settlements appear to have been largely excluded.

Area focus 1: the northern frontier

The characteristic village form on the northern frontier both north and south of Hadrian's Wall is a site of typically less than an acre (0.4 ha) in size, defined by a boundary wall enclosing a number of huts. Good examples of such sites were excavated by Professor George Jobey at Southernknowe (figure 11) and Greaves Ash on the northern frontier in Northumberland.

These village settlements are often very similar in form, with groups of stone-walled huts clustered within an enclosing wall or bank and arranged around a central courtyard or 'scooped' enclosure. The term 'scooped' derives from the distinctive sunken courtyards (seen at sites such as Coldsmouth Hill) which probably arose as a result of livestock being held within the enclosed area. The scooped effect may also be due to a need for additional spoil during enclosure construction.

Many of these sites produce evidence of an Iron Age origin, alongside activity dating from the second to fourth centuries AD. The economy of these sites is clearly biased towards the keeping of stock, with only limited evidence of arable cultivation of the marginal soils found in most upland areas. Typical examples of this sort of settlement lie between the rivers Tyne and Forth, where enclosed villages of round, stone-built huts represent the norm.

The reuse of previously deserted prehistoric settlement sites is suggested at Huckhoe (Northumberland), for example, where there was evidence of Iron Age occupation in the sixth century BC, with a later phase dated to the second century AD, and apparently lasting into the early medieval period. Huckhoe may be regarded as a fairly typical example of a 'courtyard' village, with an enclosure wall surrounding a cluster of round stone-built houses. At Southernknowe some of the houses were built into the enclosure wall (figure 11). Similar sites were common in this region between the second and fourth centuries, as at Greaves Ash (Northumberland).

South of the Roman military road running to the outpost fort at High Rochester, north of Hadrian's Wall, a number of settlements of rectangular rather than circular form have been identified, possibly suggesting a degree of Roman influence. Examples such as Birtley (Northumberland) had four or five huts fronting cobbled yards and are

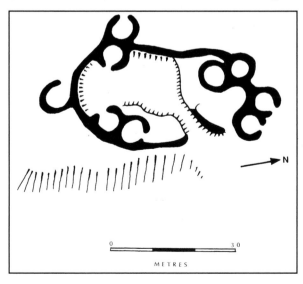

11. Simplified plan of the settlement at Southernknowe, Northumberland. (After Jobey)

normally of first- or second-century date. Professor Jobey suggested that these villages might represent official Roman development of the 'buffer' area immediately north of Hadrian's Wall, between the province and the anti-Roman Caledonian tribes to the north. This argument is supported by the identification of over forty such villages within 20 miles (32 km) of the frontier line. In the North Tyne valley excavated rectilinear enclosures have indicated the replacement of wooden huts and palisades of Iron Age type with stone houses and enclosure walls during the second century AD. It has been noted that a similar combination of circular and rectangular settlement forms also exists in north Wales, suggesting that other factors may have contributed to the form of the settlement enclosure.

Evidence relating to the economic life of these villages suggests a highly localised regional rural economy, with the likely exception of the Romanised fort-side settlements. The large number of spindle whorls found indicates that weaving was practised and also demonstrates the presence of sheep in the village economy. Small-scale metalworking is also recorded, with finds of waste slag made during excavations at Huckhoe. The primarily pastoral nature of these settlements is clear from the many finds of sheep and cattle bones, and the presence of yards and enclosures also suggests that the keeping of livestock was a vital element in the village economy. A limited level of crop cultivation is suggested by finds of the quern stones used for grinding flour. The study of plant pollen from the area shows that widespread forest clearances took place, enlarging the amount of available land to accommodate an increase in the local population, which appears to have been centred in these village settlements.

It is useful to contrast these 'native' village settlements with the frontier fort-side sites at Housesteads and Chesterholm (figure 10). The legal status as *vici* of the fort-side sites is clear from inscriptions and, as a category of site, they have much more in common with the small towns encountered in the lowland zone. They presumably fulfilled an important marketing function for the soldiers and their families based in and around the forts, but the nature of their relationship with the non-Romanised settlements within their immediate area is far from clear. What cannot be doubted is that these fort-side villages were centres of industrial activity and provided a range of specialist services to both the garrison community and visitors to the area. At Chesterholm, for example, there was an inn-like building (*mansio*) servicing the needs of travellers. Clearly, for such fort-side sites to prosper in the largely un-Romanised upland zone, a continuous army presence was necessary. In other remoter parts of the province, however, this continued military presence was not needed.

12. The round on Tregonning Hill, Cornwall, associated with Castle Pencaire hillfort beyond. (Photograph: University of Cambridge copyright reserved)

Area focus 2: Cornwall

In the far south-west of Britain lay the tribal area of *Dumnonia,* which was amongst the poorest regions of the province. Cornwall appears to have been one of the areas least affected by the arrival of either Roman administration or the forces of Romanisation, and it therefore demonstrates a far greater degree of Iron Age continuity than many other upland areas. As in the north, this continuity of Iron Age traditions may be directly attributed to a lack of Romanising influences – something confirmed by the identification of only one villa site within the whole Cornish peninsula – and the large number of small enclosed settlements of prehistoric type. The nearest centre of Roman urbanisation was far away at Exeter (*Isca Dumnoniorum*) and Cornwall generally appears to have been something of a Roman provincial backwater.

As on the northern frontier, a large number of enclosed village settlements continued largely unaltered from the pre-Roman period. Chysauster (figure 8) represents well the continuity from the Iron Age into the second century. This 'nucleated' village consisted of at least eight very similar courtyard houses and is comparable in form to sites found in Northumberland but very different from a typical Romano-British rural settlement.

It is often difficult to distinguish between the Iron Age and the Roman period in Cornwall owing to the apparently unaltered form of many village settlement sites. The best example of such continuity of site form is provided by the distinctive Cornish 'rounds' (figure 12). Although this type of settlement is Iron Age in origin, a number of examples appear to have been constructed after the Roman conquest. The typical round consisted of a circular bank and ditch enclosing a settlement area and was largely non-defensive in nature. There is a great variety of site forms of this type, including large examples such as Carvossa and Trevisker.

The absence of the Romanised settlement forms of villa and town within Cornwall, combined with the prehistoric character of many of the villages, enables a comparison to be made between Cornwall and the village sites of the northern frontier examined above. One contrast with the northern frontier is that Cornwall was unable to reap the benefits associated with being part of a long-standing military zone (even the small fort at Nanstallon was occupied only for a short period). The area therefore lacked the economic stimulus which the presence of the army brought to an area and which, in the north, led to the development of large fort-side settlements at Housesteads and Chesterholm. *Dumnonia* was probably both a political and a cultural backwater in the minds of Roman provincial administrators.

Despite the limited nature of the military presence in Cornwall, Roman authority within the region is indicated by finds of milestones. Imperial interest in Cornwall was no doubt partly due to the area's valuable tin reserves. Cornish tin production in the Roman period probably reached a peak during the third and fourth centuries, as the supply of imported metal from other provinces dwindled. The main demand for tin came from the pewter industry, itself filling a gap in the market brought about by a reduction in the imports of fine silver vessels. It is likely that, as with the Roman lead mines on the Mendips in Somerset, villages would have grown up beside the main tin extraction sites, regardless of whether the mines were worked under direct imperial control or not. Detecting such sites is, however, difficult as more recent mining operations have frequently targeted the same deposits (as they did at the Mendip lead-mining settlement at Charterhouse).

6
Smaller lowland villages

Within the lowland zone of the province lie many sites that may be usefully described as 'smaller villages'. These settlements usually exhibit a number of elements of Romanisation, including building form and construction, site layout, improved agricultural techniques, and finds indicating active participation in the Roman money-based economy. Such finds might include small numbers of Roman coins, bronze brooches, rings, pins and other cosmetic items. Sherds of fine samian ware would also be expected: this pottery was imported from Gaul during the first and second centuries; in the later Roman period it was replaced by the fine wares of British manufacture which appeared in great profusion during the third and fourth centuries, including the products of pottery centres such as the Nene Valley (figure 39), Oxfordshire and the New Forest.

The sites under consideration in this chapter are clearly different from the upland 'native' village settlements discussed in the previous chapter, partly because of a more amenable lowland position combined with more direct contact with Roman cultural and economic influences. Despite such trappings of Romanisation, however, these settlements were essentially agriculturally based and often located off the major

13. Excavations at Throckenholt, Cambridgeshire, showing part of the ditch system, filled with later peat deposits. (Photograph: copyright Cambridgeshire County Council Archaeological Field Unit)

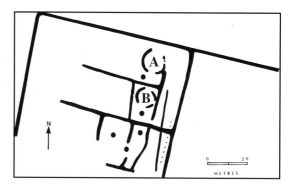

14. Plan of the site at Brockworth, Gloucestershire, in the first to the mid second century. 'A' and 'B' are the circular buildings of the Roman period. Dots indicate location of later buildings set within rectilinear plots. A line of fence posts follows one of the boundary ditches. (After Rawes)

roadways. It is likely, therefore, that they were of economic significance in strictly local terms only.

The majority of the linked compounds recognised from aerial photography and described by Sylvia Hallam around the Wash in south Lincolnshire represent typical examples of these small settlements. Excavation of the site at Throckenholt in Cambridgeshire (figure 13) revealed evidence of a complex of features, including domestic buildings and farming enclosures, all linked together by droveways which wound through the surrounding countryside.

These Romanised village settlements were normally, but not exclusively, characterised by the adoption of the rectangular building form. During the first and second centuries such buildings tended to be timber, based on footings of either sill beam or sill wall construction. By the third and fourth centuries buildings were normally being constructed of stone. Roofing materials would have included thatch (see figures 1 and 29), clay tiles and stone tiles. It is also possible that mud was used as a building material, as suggested by Sylvia Hallam with regard to settlement sites around the Wash. On a number of sites the buildings were quite fine, even featuring the use of window glass. Other buildings probably served as industrial workshops, as was the case at the later Roman pewter- and iron-making site at Little Down, near Bath.

Continuity in building traditions from the Iron Age is suggested on a number of sites, including Brockworth near Gloucester (figures 14–16), where roundhouses were constructed within the context of a settlement laid out into more Romanised rectilinear plots. These roundhouses were replaced by rectangular buildings during the second century. The development of rectilinear enclosures within Romanised settlements as seen at Brockworth is mirrored elsewhere, such as at Little Paxton (Cambridgeshire), where curvilinear enclosures of Iron Age date were also observed.

A number of these smaller village sites contained small wayside

15. Part of one of the circular buildings with associated ditch at Brockworth. (Photograph: B. Rawes)

temples constructed to house shrines dedicated to either Roman or Romano-Celtic gods. As in the urban centres, it appears that country dwellers were quick to adopt foreign deities within their rural communities. At the Portway site, also close to the *colonia* town of Gloucester, a polygonal temple was excavated. A nearby podium

16. The settlement enclosure ditch at Brockworth, with fence-post holes to the left. (Photograph: B. Rawes)

17. Plan of the site at Portway, Gloucestershire. 'S' marks the positions of the two possible shrines, and dots indicate the location of rectangular buildings. A spread of cobbles connects the shrines to the main road running through the settlement. (After Rawes)

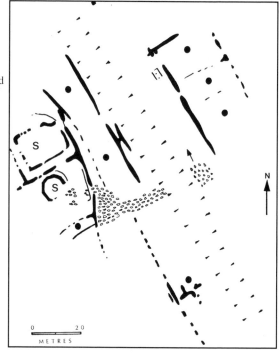

18. The polygonal shrine at Portway. (Photograph: B. Rawes)

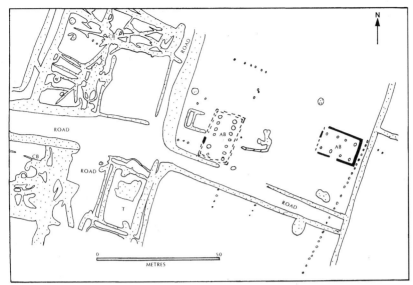

19. Plan of the site of Claydon Pike, Gloucestershire/Oxfordshire, during the second century. 'CB' (on the left) marks the cottage-type building and 'AB' (centre and right) are aisled barns. 'T' (left of centre) indicates the location of the proposed temple. (Oxford Archaeological Unit)

probably marked the site of another religious building and a carved stone head was found nearby (figures 17 and 18).

Two temples were found at the interesting site of Claydon Pike, on the upper Thames on the Gloucestershire/Oxfordshire border (figures 19–22). Excavations by the Oxfordshire Archaeological Unit revealed a square temple of Roman type close to a smaller circular stone example. The aisled building found on this site has a form that is associated with

20. View of the early Roman temple at Claydon Pike. (Photograph: Oxford Archaeological Unit)

21. Excavation of the early Roman aisled barn at Claydon Pike. (Photograph: Oxford Archaeological Unit)

the agricultural areas of some villas and was probably used for the storage of grain. The layout of the Claydon Pike settlement suggests the existence of a rudimentary street plan, with a main street or hollow way running through the village with lanes branching off at right angles. All these features were observed within the context of a well-organised landscape of small settlements, droveways and field systems. A similar street grid has been suggested at the villages of Chisenbury Warren (Wiltshire) and Dragonby (Lincolnshire). At the Portway site a cobbled lane led from the rutted main road towards the polygonal temple (figure 23).

These smaller villages were primarily agricultural in terms of their

22. General view of the excavations at Claydon Pike, showing the later Roman farm which developed in the central area of the site. (Photograph: Oxford Archaeological Unit)

23. Detail of a rutted cobbled roadway at Portway, Gloucestershire. (Photograph: B. Rawes)

economic base with the resident population probably bound closely to the land. This is clear from the frequency with which these settlements can be observed within the context of their surrounding fields. The fields – and the droveways that linked them – have been traced in a number of cases through aerial photography, which shows the cultivation lynchets and field boundaries far more clearly than would be possible from any ground-level survey. A good example of the results that can be obtained from systematic aerial recording is provided by Derrick Riley's identification of the 'brickwork' field systems of north Nottinghamshire, a programme which led to the excavation of the small Romano-British settlement site of Dunstan's Clump (figure 5). Comparable well-preserved Romano-British farming landscapes have been recorded around the Wash in south Lincolnshire during the programme of aerial survey carried out by the Fenland Research Committee and the Fenland Project. Clusters of small Romano-British farming communities linked by extensive droveway complexes have been identified in this area, an example being excavated at Throckenholt Farm (figure 13).

The fields associated with village settlements often take one of two main forms. The 'Celtic fields' – many of which may be pre-Roman in date – tend to be approximately square while, in contrast, the Romanised form is a rectangular strip. The difference between these two types is clear in the region of the rural settlement at Butcombe in Somerset. The excavator noted the presence of Celtic fields around both the excavated site and the contemporary site at nearby Scars Farm. To the south, however, around the Lye's Hole villa, the fields appear to be of a more

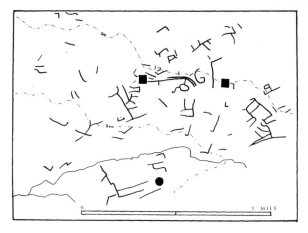

24. Plan of the field systems of 'Celtic' and Romanised type around the settlements (shown by squares) at Butcombe and Scars Farm, Somerset, and the villa at Lye's Hole (shown by the dot). (After Fowler)

Romanised strip type (figure 24). It was suggested that this might represent a degree of independence on the part of the 'native' villages, eschewing the new imported agricultural techniques used by the villa owner.

Field systems and enclosures associated with villages have been identified at a number of sites. At Chalton (Hampshire) a sizable settlement of rectangular houses occupied from the first to fourth centuries was surrounded by a large complex of fields, some of which may be pre-Roman. Similar evidence for settlement continuity was suggested at Thundersbarrow Hill in the territory of the Regni (modern Sussex and Hampshire). In this instance an extensive field system can be traced around the village, which lies outside an Iron Age hillfort (figure 25). Claydon Pike is another site lying within a complex landscape

25. Plan of the Thundersbarrow hillfort, with associated Romano-British settlement and field system. (After Cunliffe)

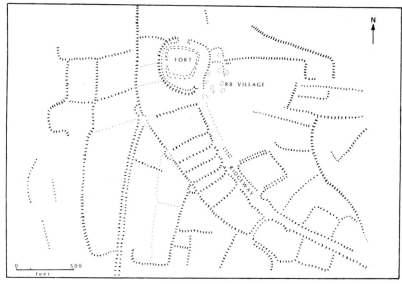

of fields, enclosures and droveways identified by aerial photography. It is clear that this whole area was covered by a dense network of nucleated village settlements and fields. Similar complex field systems have been observed in Wiltshire, at the Totterdown and Overton Down sites, while in Gloucestershire ditched field boundaries have been excavated at the villages of Brockworth and Portway (figures 14 and 17). Aerial photography has revealed further complexes of preserved Romano-British rural landscapes in the Fenlands of Cambridgeshire, Lincolnshire and Norfolk. There is also good evidence of intensive settlement activity in Wessex during the Roman period, with a mass of small settlements linked by trackways forming the focus for several village developments. Some of these villages could reach a considerable size, as in the case of Chisenbury Warren (figure 26).

Despite producing evidence of varying degrees of Romanisation, these sites should perhaps be viewed as being essentially poor and therefore bound to the land like their smaller counterparts. Many of these smaller villages appear to succeed Iron Age occupation of the same site, as already indicated for Thundersbarrow Hill and Chalton. It is possible that the site below the Thundersbarrow hillfort (figure 25) may represent the forced removal of the local population from the defended Iron Age enclosure into an open village that would have provided no potential threat to the Roman authorities. Pre-Roman settlement was also suggested at the villages of Woodcuts (Dorset), Claydon Pike and Dragonby. The last site was a very important Iron Age centre in the east Midlands, but

26. The well-preserved linear settlement at Chisenbury Warren, Wiltshire. (Photograph: University of Cambridge copyright reserved)

27. Salt-making debris (*briquetage*) from sites in the Norfolk Fens.

appears to have entered a period of decline during the Roman period. Continuity from the pre-conquest period is also suggested at such sites as Norsey Wood (Essex) and Park Brow (Sussex). The latter is of particular interest as it has produced evidence of both Bronze Age and Iron Age activity, suggesting a long history of settlement. Other smaller village sites maintained much of their Iron Age culture and were affected by the Roman conquest to only a slight degree, with Tallington (Lincolnshire) and Maxey (Cambridgeshire) being compared by their excavator to northern frontier sites such as Huckhoe.

Although agriculture was clearly of great importance to the economy of these villages, some sites produce evidence of industrial activity, occasionally on quite a large scale. In the Cambridgeshire and Norfolk Fens a number of smaller settlements produce finds of salt-making debris (*briquetage*) associated with an intensive salt industry (figure 27), an activity recorded extensively around the Wash as well as on the Red Hills of the Essex coast. Other sites produce evidence of pottery-making and metalworking. The small settlement of Little Down was involved in the large-scale industrial production of both iron and, more significantly, pewter table wares, presumably destined for the nearby prosperous town at Bath. The profits from this industrial activity, as well as those from the sale of any farming surpluses or products such as wool, leather and dairy produce, would have enabled villagers to purchase items such as fine pottery and metalwork, which were probably supplied by itinerant traders plying their wares between the isolated settlements, often located away from the main road systems.

It is possible that some of these smaller villages lay on villa estates and housed the estate workers. This may have been the case with the settlement at Lickington (Leicestershire), which lies very close to a villa building. It could also apply to the Lye's Hole villa and nearby village at Scars Farm (figure 24), and the settlement at Fotheringhay (Northamptonshire). Other villages, such as Brockworth near Gloucester, may have been situated within the *territorium* of a town. In the case of the Cambridgeshire Fenland villages, the local population may have been the tenants of the emperor himself, sited, as they probably were, on an imperial estate.

7
Village buildings

The most obviously Romanised feature in the villages of Roman Britain is the rectangular house plan, as excavated at Dragonby (Lincolnshire) (figure 7), Chalton (Hampshire) and Butcombe (Somerset) (figure 9). The widespread adoption of the rectangular form appears to have taken place during the second century, with simple and multi-functional 'strip buildings' appearing on many sites, including small towns such as *Margidunum* in Nottinghamshire (figure 45) and Water Newton in Cambridgeshire. In common with the northern frontier, rectangular buildings tend to post-date more traditional Iron Age roundhouse forms, as at Butcombe, where a second-century rectangular structure replaced a round hut of Iron Age date.

During the first and second centuries the rectangular buildings constructed on these settlements often consisted of a timber superstructure set either on a narrow sill wall or on a wooden beam laid in a shallow trench. The latter 'sill beam' method of construction is relatively easy to identify during excavation because of the beam slot, which can survive if ground conditions allow. Sill walls are less easy to identify as it can be difficult to tell whether the excavated wall is of sill type (with a timber superstructure) or merely the remaining lower courses of a wall that originally extended to the eaves of the building. In this situation much depends on the excavator's interpretation of the thickness and construction of the wall itself.

Excavations at larger village sites such as Catsgore (Somerset) and Grandford (Cambridgeshire) have revealed the plans of a number of these early timber-framed buildings. As the term 'timber-framed' suggests, the superstructure of these buildings would have been of timber, frequently used in conjunction with traditional building materials such as wattle and daub. Evidence of wall plaster is also often found. Similar buildings have been found inside a number of Roman towns.

A problem sometimes encountered in the excavation of both rural and urban sites is the identification of these early timber buildings when the earlier Roman levels in which they are usually found have been destroyed by later occupation deposits, when stone building was the norm. The rectangular stone building form became common on village sites during the third and fourth centuries, as in the case of the small industrial site of Little Down near Bath, although the form is recorded from earlier periods, as at Dragonby (figure 7). The uses to which these stone buildings were put were varied: some served as houses while others were storage places and workshops. At Little Down the rectangular stone buildings were used as workshops for the industrial production of both pewter and iron. Stone buildings found within village settlements could sometimes be well constructed, with dressed and mortared blocks and roofs of stone tiles. Thatch would have been another important roofing material although its presence is often very difficult to detect. Its use was suggested at the larger village site at Stonea in Cambridgeshire (figure 29). Clay tiles were used at many sites, particularly where stone was less readily available, as was the case in the Cambridgeshire Fens at such sites as Grandford (figure 31). It is likely, however, that clay tiles were expensive and therefore reserved for the more affluent members of the village community. The use of mud as a building material in some areas might also be expected and mud-built structures are certainly recorded during the medieval period in areas such as Nottinghamshire and Lincolnshire. Archaeological remains are tenuous at best.

Although the rectangular building plan became the normal type in lowland Britain during the Roman period, the roundhouse did not disappear altogether and a number of lowland sites have produced evidence for the continued use of wooden circular buildings of essentially Iron Age character. The sites often associated with such buildings tend to be poorer, as at East Tilbury (Essex), a site dating from the first and second centuries, where four circular huts built from timber, wattle and daub were excavated. Similar structures were excavated at Green Ore on Mendip (Somerset), where the extraction of silver from locally mined lead ore was carried out. Better appointed roundhouses have been excavated at Brockworth, close to the Roman *colonia* at Gloucester (figure 14). Excavations at that site revealed two 'eavesdrip' gullies designed to drain rainwater from the thatched roof. The Brockworth circular buildings survived into the second century, when they were replaced by rectangular timber structures. Circular stone buildings of indeterminate function are also known from Little Down.

Many small town sites have produced evidence of affluent buildings incorporating such Romanised elements as the hypocaust underfloor heating system, painted plaster walls and even glazed windows. In a number of instances these rich buildings are very similar to the villas found at the centre of farming estates within the Romano-British countryside. Such villa-type structures have been identified at a number of small town sites, including Camerton (Somerset), Water Newton (Cambridgeshire) and Kingscote (Gloucestershire). In these cases it is obviously difficult to differentiate between what may have been merely a pretentious home, inhabited by a member of the village or small town community, and a more traditional estate centre and landowner residence. Similar villa-type buildings have also been identified within major towns such as Cirencester.

A number of village and small town sites have produced evidence of unusual buildings, such as the curious polygonal structures identified at Catsgore (figure 33) and the imposing stone tower at Stonea. Both sites are discussed in detail in the following chapter.

8
Prosperous large villages

The villages examined in the previous chapters exhibit a number of Romanised features but owed much more to their Iron Age origins than to the new Roman regime, and they may in many cases be viewed as 'native' rather than 'Roman'. The settlements considered in this chapter are often of considerable size, extending over many acres. They demonstrate a far greater degree of Romanisation than any of the sites discussed above and, in archaeological terms, illustrate the economic and social benefits which participation in the economic life of the province could bring. As a result, it is not too surprising that many of these larger sites are located beside major Roman roads. Catsgore (Somerset) (figure 34) represents one of the best examples of an excavated roadside site. The investigation of this settlement revealed the remains of buildings and associated enclosures extending over a large area on both sides of the Roman road on which the village was centred.

The apparently prosperous and highly Romanised nature of these large communities is often apparent during excavation. As with smaller sites, the presence of coins indicates participation in the Roman monetary economy, but here to a far greater degree. Fine pottery wares are also frequently found, with imported samian replaced in the third and fourth centuries by local British products. The standard rectangular form of building – with many variations – is found on all these sites. At Catsgore there were simple rectangular buildings alongside examples of both aisled and apsidal-ended types, as well as villa-type buildings.

As with the small towns examined in the next chapter, it is likely that many of these villages performed an important function as a local market centre, the prosperity of which must have largely determined the development and eventual success of the settlement.

Site focus 1: the Fenlands

A detailed programme of aerial survey, field-walking and excavation in the Cambridgeshire Fens has revealed a concentration of large, prosperous and highly Romanised settlements within a comparatively small area clustering around the modern market town of March. In some parts of Fenland extensive Iron Age sea or freshwater flooding resulted in the Roman settlement pattern owing very little to earlier landscapes. In the March area, however, there is evidence of several prosperous Iron Age sites occupying the same drier ground that was later to prove attractive to Romano-British rural settlements. It is reasonable to assume that in a number of cases the occupants of these settlements were largely the same, although the evidence suggests that many of the Roman Fenland village sites did not fully develop until the early second century.

The absence of private villa estates and towns in the Fens, combined with the evidence for major investments in both communications and drainage works, has led many archaeologists to conclude that Fenland was an imperial estate. These lands would have been effectively the personal property of the Roman emperor, administered on his behalf by a local agent (*procurator saltus*). The case for this area being an imperial estate is strengthened by the extensive evidence of salt-making in Fenland during the Roman period – salt-making was an imperial monopoly (figure 27).

The absence of towns and villas means that the study of villages in this region can take place within the context of a farming landscape, where the villages are the most significant units of rural settlement.

Major excavations by Tim Potter and Ralph Jackson of the British Museum at Stonea, near March, have revealed what may have been the administrative centre of this imperial estate (figure 28). This fascinating

28. View of the excavations at Stonea Grange, Cambridgeshire, showing a north–south street, associated with a series of ditches (with later plough marks clearly visible). (Photograph: T. Potter)

29. Reconstruction drawing by Stephen Crummy showing the second-century stone tower and associated settlement at Stonea Grange. (Reproduced by permission of the Trustees of the British Museum)

settlement was established between AD 130 and 150 on what had probably been a regional centre for the Iceni tribe during the later Iron Age. The Roman village was laid out in a planned manner, with a grid of gravelled streets. There was a clear division between an eastern zone, producing evidence of domestic settlement with associated industrial activity, and a western zone, containing a stone building complex, unusual in an area where most building stone had to be imported. The site was linked by an artificial canal to a system of inland tidal waterways, which connected many of the Roman sites in the area to each other and to the sea.

The centrepiece of the western complex of stone buildings was a remarkable tower (figure 29). This probably stood three storeys high and is unique in Britain. The tower was constructed from stone brought into Fenland and was richly finished, with evidence of underfloor hypocaust heating, decorated mosaic floors, painted plaster walls, marble veneers and glazed windows. The tower was fronted by a large metalled courtyard that may have served as a market place. It is thought that this building was probably the administrative centre for the Fenland imperial estate, perhaps even providing the headquarters for the *procurator saltus* himself. The tower would also have undoubtedly acted as a beacon of Romanisation to the emerging settlements in the local area.

The eastern part of the Stonea settlement was clearly separate from the tower complex. It consisted of densely packed wooden buildings with thatched roofs and aligned on to a grid of streets. The archaeological evidence suggests that the main economic activity was the preparation of salted lamb joints for export, possibly to the Roman army garrisoned in Britain or on the continent. Connected to the site by a gravelled road

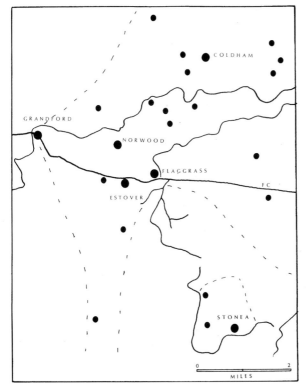

30. Large village sites in the Cambridgeshire Fens. (After Potter)

was a small temple, probably dedicated to the Roman goddess Minerva, to whom several small dedications were found.

Both the tower and temple buildings were deliberately demolished around AD 220. The excavators suggest that during the early third century Stonea's administrative role may have been taken over by the expanding Fen-edge small towns at Water Newton (*Durobrivae*) and Godmanchester (*Durovigutum*). Around this same time it has been estimated that 20 per cent of Fenland settlement sites were abandoned as a result of repeated flooding, although there is evidence of only limited flooding on the site itself.

Despite the demolition of the tower and temple complexes, the Stonea settlement continued in a less affluent and less rigidly planned form to the end of the Roman period. During the early fourth century there even appears to have been something of an economic revival, with another fine stone building constructed on the site of the earlier tower.

Four other large villages of between 25 and 40 acres (about 10–15 ha) have been located in the March area of the central Fens, all located on natural islands in the surrounding peat fen (figure 30). The sites at Flaggrass, Norwood and Grandford all lie close to the Fen Causeway, the Roman road and canal system which crossed the Fens from east to

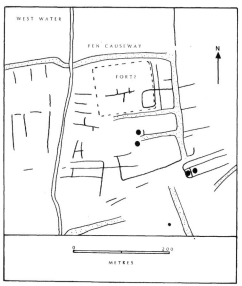

31. Simplified plan of the village site at Grandford, Cambridgeshire. The main Roman road (the Fen Causeway) follows the edge of the probable fort; a number of branching side streets lead from it. Excavated buildings are marked by dots. (After Potter)

west. These large villages provided a focus for complexes of small enclosures linked together by droveways. Most of these settlements originated or dramatically developed during the early second century, probably as a result of official impetus in the reigns of the emperors Hadrian and Antoninus Pius. At Grandford, however, there is good evidence for a mid-first-century fort, acting as an initial focus for settlement activity of a type already seen on the northern frontier (figures 31 and 32).

The impetus to settlement which appears to have occurred throughout the area during the early second century is clear at all these sites and, although much of Fenland was subject to flooding during the first half

32. Aerial photograph showing the fort and associated settlement at Grandford. (Photograph and copyright: Ben Robinson 1997)

of the third century, there is evidence of site prosperity and expansion during the late third and fourth centuries. During this period there was extensive rebuilding at Grandford, with imported stone from the east Midlands being used to construct affluent stone houses with tiled roofs, plastered and whitewashed walls and glazed windows.

Evidence of a large site engaged in the production of salt on an industrial scale has been identified close to the Fen Causeway at Norwood, beside a now silted-up tidal waterway. This site produced evidence of well-organised and extensive activity, clearly visible in finds of the crudely made, clay salt-making debris (*briquetage*) covering many acres (figure 27). Other finds included two clay-built evaporation tanks used to extract salt from the salt water collected from the tidal waterway. The evaporation process was speeded up by the use of large ovens, with locally cut peat providing a source of fuel. Large numbers of smaller villages and farmsteads were also involved in the salt-making industry, clustering along the lines of now extinct tidal watercourses. Much of this salt was probably used in the salting of meat for export, as was suggested by the excavators of Stonea.

Recent work in the Fens has dispelled the traditional view that this was one of the principal arable centres of the province. It is now clear that the pastoral economy was more important, with a number of sites producing evidence for the rearing of both sheep and cattle. Animal bone studies indicate that sheep were of the greater importance in the region, with the age of the bones indicating that animals were often kept for their wool rather than for their meat, although at Stonea there was clear evidence for the slaughtering of sheep at a young age and for the preparation of salted joints. Such joints were probably destined for export to other parts of the province or empire, and some may have been intended for the military garrisons of Roman Britain.

Site focus 2: Catsgore

The excavation at Catsgore in Somerset is one of the most important pieces of work yet undertaken on a lowland Roman roadside village, and the site therefore merits special consideration. The settlement (figure 34) represents another good example of a large and fairly prosperous village, comparable to the Fenland sites. The first major developments on the site occurred during the second century AD, with the construction of a number of curious polygonal buildings of timber-framed construction based on narrow sill walls (figure 33). Each lay in separate embanked enclosures or compounds, which the excavator has suggested indicate individual farming complexes. During the second, third and fourth centuries these units developed, with polygonal buildings replaced by stone-built structures of various types. Some of these buildings were

33. Early Roman buildings at Catsgore, Somerset, including a polygonal structure. (After Leech)

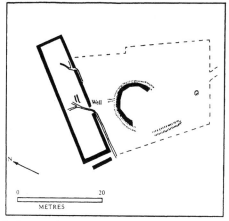

thought to be domestic, while others may have had an agricultural function. The apsidal-ended buildings are one of the more curious features of the site. In the fourth century the earth boundaries of the enclosures were removed and replaced in stone, illustrating the continued observance of historic boundaries. The organised settlement to the west of the Roman road contrasts with that to the east, revealed primarily by geophysical survey. Here there were no separate enclosures and the occupation pattern appears to have been of a much more organic and random nature.

The site at Catsgore may usefully be compared with other linear settlements incorporating individual farming compounds, including the excavated site at Hibaldstow (Lincolnshire), where a number of separate properties or plots were identified in the context of a roadside development.

34. Simplified plan of the site at Catsgore, Somerset, in the fourth century. Note the large village-type building and the location of other buildings set within ditched, banked or walled enclosures. (After Leech)

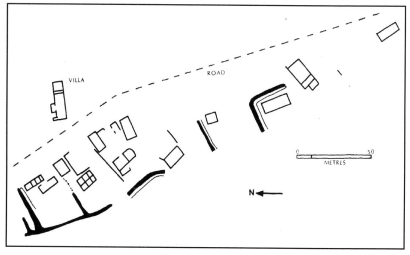

9
Small towns

Site form

A number of the sites which fall within the vast cross-section of larger villages or local urbanised centres within the Romano-British countryside have been grouped together under the rather unsatisfactory heading of 'small town' (see chapter 2). It is also possible that the Latin term *vicus* may be applied to a number of these settlements, but the meaning of this title is controversial.

The sites falling into the category of small town may be described as essentially large roadside settlements that provided a range of specialist services to road users while, at the same time, utilising their position near to road (or waterway) systems to facilitate the distribution of local industrial and agricultural products. It is also likely that in some instances these sites performed a limited role in local provincial administration. Small town sites do not tend to be found in areas of the province where towns and villas did not develop. They therefore represent a wholly Romanised site form.

Not all small towns are positioned on major Roman roads such as the Fosse Way and Watling Street. Many lie on less important routes which can no longer be traced, as in the cases of the large sites of Wycomb and Kingscote in the Gloucestershire Cotswolds

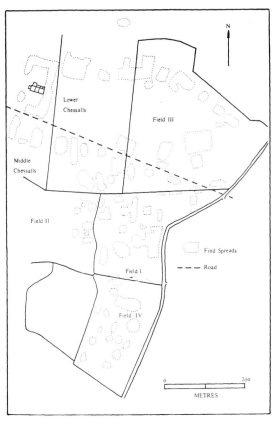

35. The large spread of finds across the site at Kingscote, Gloucestershire. (After RCHM)

(figures 35 and 36) and Kelvedon in Essex.

Although there is reasonably common agreement that sites designated as 'small towns' should have a settlement area extending over at least 25 acres (10 ha), unfortunately this benchmark is applied inconsistently, with settlement areas defined by defensive walls exhibiting a considerable variation in size. At Ancaster (Lincolnshire) the walled area extends to only 10 acres (4 ha), whereas at Godmanchester (Cambridgeshire) the defences enclose 27 acres (11 ha). At Water Newton (Cambridgeshire) the defences of the small town of *Durobrivae* enclose some 44 acres (17 ha), with good evidence for extensive settlement beyond the defended

36. Plan of Lawrence's 1864 excavations at Wycomb, Gloucestershire. Note the temple building (15) and the curving wall of the suggested theatre (5). Compare with figure 47. (RCHM(E): Crown copyright)

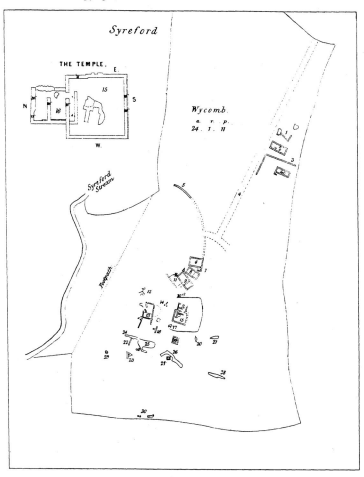

circuit covering an area at least seven times as large. Such extramural activity is a feature of many defended small town sites, where the walled area often appears to bear little relation to the total extent of the settlement. Such figures for site size may be contrasted with those for the official tribal (*civitas*) capital of the Iceni at Caistor-by-Norwich (*Venta Icenorum*) (Norfolk) at 35 acres (14 ha). Similar diversity is encountered when considering undefended small town sites, a good example being Kingscote, which covered an estimated 100 acres (40 ha). However, the small towns discussed here are generally smaller than the larger urban centres, such as Colchester at 108 acres (44 ha) and Cirencester at 250 acres (100 ha).

Despite such differences in size, the main factor that distinguishes small towns from the *coloniae* and *civitas* capitals is the lack of evidence at most sites for the imposition of any planned settlement layout based around the familiar *insulae* street grid system. As a direct result, small towns tend to exhibit a more organic growth pattern, with building densities that are certainly not as great as those found within the planned urban foundations. This more random street plan development is clear at such sites as Water Newton (Cambridgeshire) and Camerton (Somerset). The density of site occupation clearly has implications for any estimated population levels. A straight comparison between planned towns and more organic small towns based on site acreage alone is therefore inappropriate.

The lack of planning in both foundation and development represents the main difference between small towns and the major urban centres. Despite their size and defences, the former remain village-type settlements of essentially rural character. The ribbon-pattern development of many roadside settlements, such as those at Wimpole in Cambridgeshire, Hibaldstow in Lincolnshire and Kenchester in Herefordshire (figure 37), has much in common with the familiar linear village plan of the medieval period.

In addition to a planned street grid, a number of other features characterise what may be described as 'true towns'. These include major public buildings such as baths and temples, as well as the forum/basilica complexes normally found at the centre of Roman urban settlements. A number of the more developed small towns do possess some of these features: at Godmanchester there was evidence of a baths complex associated with a *mansio* and an early-third-century basilica-type building, while at Water Newton there were probably both a *mansio* and a high-status administrative block.

Site origins

Many small towns produce evidence for an Iron Age origin. Within the author's study area of Gloucestershire and Somerset, of 136 sites identified, over 35 per cent revealed some form of evidence of Iron Age activity. In the context of Roman Britain as a whole, it has been suggested that over 25 per cent of small town sites produce some form of evidence of pre-existing Iron Age settlement activity, with a much greater proportion in the south and east of the province.

In Oxfordshire the sites of Frilford and Lower Lea produced good evidence of Iron Age activity, with the latter located close to a prehistoric hillfort. A significant pre-Roman presence is also suggested at Ancaster, although the comparable walled site at *Margidunum* in Nottinghamshire (figure 45) produced no such indications. In the territory of the Trinovantes a number of small towns have produced evidence for an Iron Age settlement origin, with the possible failed tribal capital of Chelmsford (Essex) being the only major exception. Kelvedon was an important Iron Age trading centre, as were Braintree and Harlow (Essex). At Heybridge (Essex) large numbers of *amphorae* sherds may indicate trading contacts with Roman merchants in the pre-conquest period, although recent work has questioned assertions that Heybridge was the site of a thriving river port. Braughing (Hertfordshire) was sufficiently prosperous in the pre-Roman period to mint its own coins. Rochester and Springhead (Kent) were both important Iron Age centres, the former on a crossing point of the river Medway and the latter a likely religious centre.

Other small towns appear to have originated as fort-side settlements, comparable to the examples discussed in chapter 5 on the northern frontier at sites such as Housesteads and Chesterholm in Northumberland. As in the north, such settlements tended to grow up close to the fort gates. In this context it is worth remembering that during the conquest

37. The small town at Kenchester, Herefordshire. Note the dense network of side streets branching from the main road, the outer defences and the outlines of numerous buildings. (Photograph: University of Cambridge copyright reserved)

period forts would have represented the most valuable focus of trade in an area, because of the unique spending power of the resident troops, whose pay formed the basis for the province's monetary economy. These fort-side settlements therefore attracted merchants and artisans, as well as the soldiers' families, who were forced to live outside the fort defences. Retired veterans from the fort's garrison may have resided within these settlements, thereby increasing their wealth. These sites would also have benefited economically from their strategic military location on major road junctions or river crossings. It has been estimated that around 35 per cent of small town sites originated with the construction of a fort, with nearer 70 per cent of sites in the more militarised north and west of the province having such roots.

At Godmanchester the ditches and rampart of one of a series of forts along the Great Ouse have been revealed. At Chelmsford finds included military equipment, Claudian pottery of the mid first century and early timber buildings of military type, all probably from a conquest-period fort on that site. Other small towns with probable fort origins include *Margidunum* (Nottinghamshire), Sea Mills (Bristol), Catterick and Malton (North Yorkshire), Mancetter (Warwickshire), Mildenhall (Wiltshire), Water Newton (Cambridgeshire), Wall (Staffordshire) and Alchester (Oxfordshire). In some cases small towns could have both an Iron Age and a military origin, a situation suggested at sites such as Ancaster (Lincolnshire) and Dorchester-on-Thames (Oxfordshire).

Site economy

The essentially agricultural nature of many small town sites is clear,

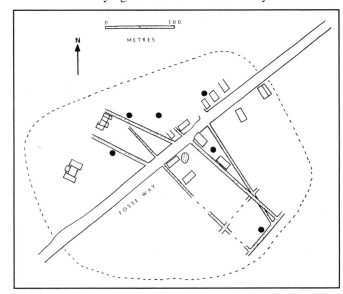

38. Simplified plan of Camerton, Somerset. The dots indicate further buildings. Note the two winged corridor villa-type buildings to the north of the Fosse Way and the simple grid of side streets. (After Wedlake)

39. Pottery from the Nene Valley kilns near Peterborough.

despite their size and common prosperity. The large site at God-manchester provides a good example. Behind the main street frontages the excavators discovered evidence for a number of farming plots incorporating a range of small agricultural structures, including drying racks for corn and grain storage pits. Survey work in the local area has revealed the large field system that surrounded and supported this extensive settlement. Paddocks and plots are also recorded on the periphery of the extensive roadside settlement at Wimpole near Cambridge and inside the site at Braintree (Essex). During the third and fourth centuries Camerton on the Fosse Way (figure 38) was the focus of a thriving pewter industry supplying its products to customers throughout the West Country. Nevertheless, there was still strong evidence of agricultural activity, in the form of tools for cultivation as well as in finds associated with corn milling, and the spinning and weaving of wool.

These settlements clearly played an important role within the province as vital centres for both industrial production and distribution. A number of likely small town sites have produced interesting evidence relating to the industrial production of pottery, as seems to have been the case at Mancetter. The distinctive Nene Valley fine wares (figure 39) were produced in over seventy individual kiln sites clustered beside the extensive small town at Water Newton (*Durobrivae*) and over 130 kiln sites have been found in an industrial zone of the small town of Brampton (Norfolk). The large site at Congresbury (Somerset) was the centre of a distinctive local grey ware industry, with many separate kiln sites located during excavations.

Evidence of industrial metalworking is also frequently encountered at sites such as Camerton (Somerset) and Nettleton (Wiltshire), associated with the pewter tableware industry which flourished in the third and fourth centuries. Both sites contained rectangular stone workshops and produced finds of pewter-making slag and the moulds used in the production process. The products of this industry were widely distributed, representing relatively common finds on villa sites in the region. At Nettleton this industrial activity appears to have replaced a temple complex dedicated to Apollo as the main economic basis of the settlement. It is also worth noting that Camerton revealed much evidence of farming activity during the third and fourth centuries, in tandem with the development of the pewter and iron industries at that site. At Braughing bronze and iron goods were produced during the third century,

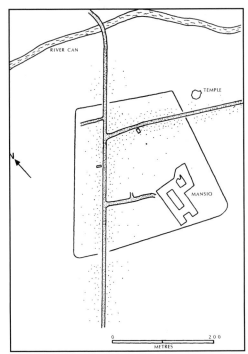

40. Simplified plan of the probable small town at Chelmsford, Essex, showing the spread of roadside settlement.

while at Malton an inscription indicates the presence of a goldsmith. At Charterhouse (Somerset) there is evidence of what may be imperially owned primary production associated with lead mining and silver extraction. On a more domestic scale, excavations at Wimpole Hall (Cambridgeshire) produced evidence of the no doubt typically localised industries of leather and bone working.

It has been suggested that the majority of small towns were self-supporting in the everyday products of grain, meat and dairy produce, as well as in the basic necessities, such as cloth, tools and some of the coarser pottery wares found at these sites. This is not likely to have been the case with the true urban centres. The major towns of Roman Britain are often viewed as being economically parasitic on the countryside surrounding them, unable to produce all the food and other essentials required by those who lived within the town walls. In this economic sense town and small town may be seen as fundamentally different. The major towns were wholly urban and specialised in the production of fine manufactured goods and the provision of the range of specialist services indicated by the presence of baths, temples, markets and administrative buildings. By contrast, most small towns were essentially rural: villages whose size was due largely to the economic stimulus provided by the Roman road system. The small towns appear to have been a direct result of the marketing potential offered by the Roman roads and the development of the new and valuable markets created by the towns and villas. To that extent, small towns were essentially artificial creations and therefore wholly Roman institutions.

The economic importance of these small town sites is clear, with many serving as market centres for their local area, assuming that most rural populations needed to travel to market and back in a single day.

41. The distribution of coastal settlements along the Severn estuary.

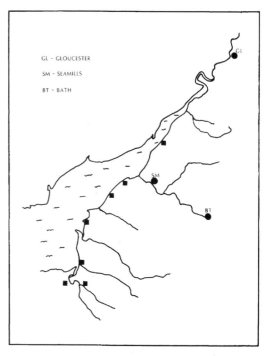

GL - GLOUCESTER

SM - SEAMILLS

BT - BATH

This localised market function is also suggested by the many villas found clustering around these settlements, such as at Water Newton, Kingscote, Ancaster, Braughing and Rochester. It remains possible, however, that in some instances the settlement was actually under direct villa ownership. Smaller non-villa farmsteads also cluster around these sites, as was the case at Godmanchester. The size and relative affluence of the small town settlement presumably indicate its degree of success as a market centre.

Some of these small towns appear to have been ports. The existence of inland ports has been suggested at Ilchester (Somerset) and at Chelmsford (figure 40), where there were possible wharves recorded by the riverside. The distribution of likely small town sites on the east coast of the Severn estuary indicates the presence of possible port sites at regular intervals (figure 41). At Sea Mills (Bristol) and Bawdrip (Somerset) there was evidence of dockside warehouses, as well as a considerable level of trade in commodities transported in *amphorae*. These would have included olive oil, wine and fish sauce (*garum*), imported into Roman Britain mainly from Gaul and Spain.

It is likely that, as with comparable settlements during the medieval period, Romano-British small towns and villages hosted weekly markets and larger seasonal fairs, which presumably attracted interest over a much wider area than did the smaller weekly markets. Weekly markets were no doubt used for the sale of perishable foodstuffs while at seasonal fairs corn, livestock and manufactured goods might be bought and sold. Farmstead and villa owners living close to a small town might visit the settlement's market or fair in order to sell surplus arable or livestock produce and to buy cattle or manufactured goods like fine pottery or iron tools. These goods might well be produced in the settlement itself or be made available by itinerant merchants, who probably also served as middlemen to supply products to the nearest urban centre. Such merchants (*negotiatores*) are recorded on inscriptions in Gaul. It has been estimated that locally based market trade accounted for over three-quarters of Roman economic exchange. Elsewhere in the empire fairs were of particular importance to the economic life of primarily agricultural provinces. Writing about Antioch, Libanius observed that 'many large villages ... have craftsmen as in towns and exchange their products with one another through fairs'. There may also have been a link between rural fairs and religious festivals, a relationship recorded elsewhere in the empire.

Site development
It is clear that the small towns represent a direct response to the marketing potential offered by the new Roman road and waterway systems, which presented opportunities that would probably have been recognised by those living in existing prehistoric settlements. In the counties of Gloucestershire and Somerset, out of ninety-three probable small towns and villages identified by the author, some fifty-nine were located beside a major Roman road. This is a telling statistic.

A useful example of the economic impetus that the Roman road system could bring to the development of rural communities is provided by the site at Bourton (Gloucestershire). Although many sites originated as fort-side settlements, it was economic factors that caused them to develop and flourish. At Bourton the local settlement appears to have relocated from an Iron Age centre at Salmondsbury hillfort. This fort was located on the Jurassic Way, the ancient trackway running along the Cotswold ridge. Following the construction of the Fosse Way some thousand yards (900 metres) to the west and the creation of a crossing point over the nearby river Windrush, there was a population shift towards the new road, which replaced the Jurassic Way as the most important economic artery in the region. This movement of an existing Iron Age population is suggested by the continued use of some pottery forms and the fact that the new Roman settlement area stretched back into the hillfort, which was linked to the Fosse Way by a metalled track. The small town site that developed at Bourton eventually extended over an estimated area of 30 acres (12 ha) and took the form of a ribbon development

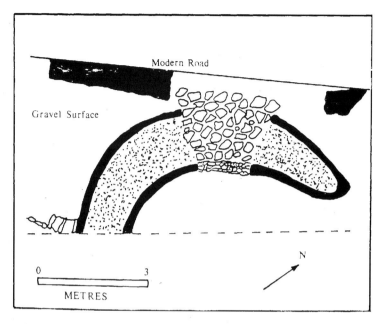

Modern Road

Gravel Surface

N

0   3

METRES

42. Possible small temple building at Bourton, Gloucestershire. (After O'Neil)

stretching along both sides of a river crossing on the Fosse Way, with evidence of the existence of a rudimentary metalled street plan.

Buildings found during excavations at Bourton included an apse-ended 'wayside shrine' (figure 42), an industrial building with forge and ovens, a probable bakehouse and a row of open-fronted shops. There was also evidence suggesting the existence of a posting station (*mansio*) on the site. This range of buildings presumably existed to provide road users with all the services they might require on their travels, including a bed for the night. The location of the settlement 15 miles (24 km) from the major town of Cirencester to the south-west would have made Bourton a popular stopping point for travellers using the Fosse Way. The affluence that these travellers brought to the site is clear from the richly finished houses on the site, incorporating features such as mosaic floors and underfloor heating.

The site of Springhead in Kent appears to have a similar ribbon development to that at Bourton, as does Godmanchester, where a crossing over the river Ouse provided the focus for settlement development. The extensive site at Wimpole Hall in Cambridgeshire stretched for about a kilometre along the roadside at a major junction of Ermine Street and Akeman Street, while comprehensive excavations at Hibaldstow revealed a similar ribbon development focused on Ermine Street.

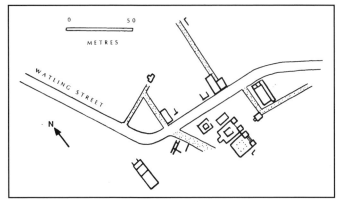

43. Simplified plan of the large roadside temple complex at Springhead, Kent, on Watling Street. (After Detsicas)

The development of a rudimentary street plan as at Bourton has been noted at a number of other sites, in each instance suggesting a degree of internal settlement organisation and planning. This planning is not comparable with the *insulae* grid system of urban centres like Silchester, but basic settlement organisation is suggested at sites such as Kenchester (figure 37), Water Newton, Godmanchester, Chelmsford (figure 40), Camerton, Springhead and Dorn (Gloucestershire). A plan of Camerton (figure 38) clearly shows that some of the settlement buildings were located facing the Fosse Way, which ran through the settlement, while others were aligned along the metalled side streets. The layout of streets at Alchester does, however, suggest the existence of a pre-planned – rather than organic – site grid system, something also suggested at the small towns of Braughing and Catterick.

In some instances the streets within a small town were the focus for intensive settlement activity along the main frontages, normally taking the form of multi-function rectangular strip buildings located within thin plots. The site at Water Newton is a good example of this sort of dense settlement pattern.

Specialised buildings

The provision of services to travellers, especially those connected with the operation of the Imperial Post (*cursus publicus*), is suggested by the number of posting stations (*mansiones*) such as that at Godmanchester. Here a *mansio* was established around AD 120, linked to a baths and temple complex. A large *mansio* was also excavated at Chelmsford (figure 40) and the existence of similar buildings has been suggested at sites such as Bourton, Wall, Towcester (Northamptonshire) and Water Newton. Posting stations provided overnight accommodation

54

44. Probable temple buildings III and XVI of later-second-century date excavated at Camerton, Somerset. (After Wedlake)

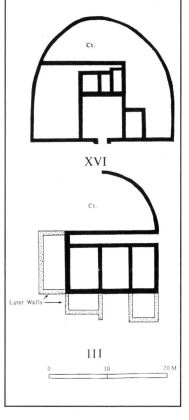

and stabling and may be compared to the roadside inns of later times. It is possible that some villages were legally bound to provide services for users of the main roads, as was the case in other provinces.

Religious buildings for use by travellers, pilgrims and locals were provided at a number of small town sites, including Springhead, Nettleton, Frilford, Wycomb, Godmanchester and Bourton (figure 42). At Springhead (figure 43) a large religious complex incorporating a temple and baths lay alongside Watling Street, between Canterbury and London. On this site a large walled temple area was constructed during the second century. It had an entrance building and was fitted out with fine mosaic floors and painted plaster walls. The siting of this temple complex was probably due to the presence of springs at the site. In this sense Springhead is similar to the great spring-based temple site in the town of Bath. In some instances temples are associated with theatre buildings, as suggested at Wycomb (figure 36) and Bath. Such buildings were presumably connected to the religious life of the temples.

Some of the largest religious small town complexes may be compared to similar sites identified in Roman Gaul and termed *conciliabula*. These Gallic settlements have a range of monumental buildings, including baths, temples and theatres, lying within the context of a large rural settlement (figure 47).

A number of small town sites have produced evidence of the existence of fine villa-type buildings of a sort normally found on private farming estates in the countryside. At Camerton (figures 38 and 44) excavations revealed two 'winged corridor' villa-type buildings, both located within the settlement and contemporary with it. The buildings featured mosaic floors, painted plaster walls and well-sculpted architectural fragments. Other fine town or villa-type buildings have been excavated at Great

Chesterford (Essex), Kenchester, Braughing and *Margidunum*. Because such buildings so closely resemble typical villas, some archaeologists have suggested that they represent the houses of 'traditional' villa estate owners, who both founded and owned the associated rural settlement. There are certainly examples of large villas lying at probable villa estates in the traditional sense, as for example at Rivenhall (Essex) and Westland (Somerset). At Kingscote in Gloucestershire (figure 35) a very large villa-type building complex lies behind an extensive small town.

Villa-type buildings are increasingly identified with the major Roman towns such as Cirencester, making it likely that the villas at sites such as Camerton and *Margidunum* indicate the presence within a settlement of people who were merely sufficiently affluent to build themselves large and luxurious houses.

Local administration

As will be discussed further in chapter 11, it is likely that some small towns served as centres for the administration of their local tribal area (*pagus*), in some cases probably housing local officials such as the *centurio regionarius* recorded at Bath, who may have been involved in the local collection of taxes in kind (*annona*), and the *beneficiarius consularis* from Dorchester, who may have had a local policing role. At Irchester (Northamptonshire) a tombstone of a member of the governor's official mobile staff (*stratores consulares*) has been found.

It has been suggested that Water Newton was elevated to the status of a *civitas* capital by the start of the fourth century and that the substantial villa or palace complex constructed close to the edge of the settlement at Castor (Cambridgeshire) in AD *c*.300 was built for an important provincial official. A possible *basilica* building for use by a local council was constructed at Godmanchester during the early third century.

Peter Salway has suggested that in those tribal areas (*civitates peregrinae*) where there was no principal town, there was instead a 'rural network' of small towns and village-type communities. This would certainly appear to be the case across significant parts of areas such as Somerset and Cambridgeshire, where major towns are absent.

Defences

In the later Roman period defences were constructed at many small town sites, presumably as part of a wider provincial scheme that exploited the strategic position behind the economic success of many of these settlements. The first of these defences were simple earthwork circuits erected at a number of sites by the end of the second century, including *Margidunum* (figure 45), Water Newton, Irchester, Rochester and Chelmsford (figure 40). Stone defences were constructed at many sites

45. Plan of the defended small town at *Margidunum*, Nottinghamshire, on the Fosse Way. (After Todd)

FOSSE WAY

0   200

METRES

during the late second and third centuries, as at Godmanchester, Towcester and Rochester, apparently as part of a general programme of fortification undertaken at this time in the majority of towns in Britain. Work continued on many small town defences during the fourth century, with a number of pre-existing circuits further strengthened by the addition of external towers. These fourth-century works are probably linked to the defensive initiatives in Britain of Count Theodosius.

The fortification of small towns was far from a uniform policy, however, and a number of large sites remained undefended. Such was the case at the 80 acre (32 ha) site of Kingscote (figure 35), as well as at Braughing, Springhead, Maidstone and Lower Lea. It is likely that small towns were defended, not out of imperial concern for the safety of their occupants, but rather as part of a provincial defensive scheme. Many small towns originated as fort-side settlements and inherited a strategic position. This provincial plan may have resulted in the creation of a series of fortified posts scattered throughout the countryside along the major routes of communication, as on the Fosse Way at Dorn, Ancaster and *Margidunum*. Many sites close to the Fosse Way were, however, left undefended, as at Camerton and Kingscote. A number of defended small towns also lay along the London to Chichester road, at sites such as Hardham (West Sussex), but the large 70 acre (24 ha) site at Ewell (Surrey) remained undefended. Likewise on the Canterbury to London road, Rochester was defended but Springhead was not.

Open spaces are recorded within some of the defended circuits, such as those identified at *Margidunum* and Alchester. These may reflect their use by the later Roman field army, again indicating that the defences were not there necessarily for the benefit of the local population.

10
Later Roman villages

There is nothing to suggest a great decline in the fortunes of Romano-British village settlements during the fourth century. On the contrary, in the earlier part of the century, there is considerable evidence for a high level of prosperity at many sites, as in the Cambridgeshire Fens and at the industrially based sites at Camerton in Somerset (figure 38) and Little Down near Bath.

All these settlements appear to have benefited from the economic boom recorded throughout the province during the early fourth century, which also affected many town and villa sites. The villa estates appear to have enjoyed their period of greatest prosperity at this time, something very apparent in the large villa complexes of south-east and south-west England. Differential prosperity becomes apparent as the fourth century develops, with major towns like Cirencester prospering but centres such as Leicester and Wroxeter entering a period of decline. Such a contrast is also apparent at a number of village sites. In Sussex and Hampshire there is a confused situation, with sites like Park Brow (Sussex) being abandoned, while others like Chalton (Hampshire) demonstrate evidence of marked development. At Godmanchester there was decline and abandonment at this time. Settlements in upland areas appear to have been affected only slightly by the Roman conquest and things probably changed little at the ending of Roman control, with sites like Huckhoe (Northumberland) demonstrating a degree of continuity into the early medieval period.

A problem which besets any attempt to identify clear evidence for continuity of settlement is the difficulty of demonstrating continuous occupation where later settlements occupy the same sites as Roman ones. Evidence of Roman occupation on a Dark Age or medieval site does not necessarily mean continuous habitation. This is particularly true where Roman villages occupy a prime location, for example a river crossing, that might also have attracted later settlement activity. A useful example is provided by the deserted medieval village site at Upton (Gloucestershire), which produced Roman remains (figure 46). Was there continuous settlement, or had the Roman site been long deserted by the time the medieval village was founded? Finds of Saxon pottery might weight the arguments towards continuity.

Some form of continuity is, however, suggested at a number of sites. There is evidence of early Germanic settlement at Heybridge and Rivenhall (Essex), and at Chelmsford (Essex) the lack of evidence of German settlement during the fifth and sixth centuries may indicate the

46. The location of Roman finds on the site of the deserted medieval village at Upton, Gloucestershire. (After Rahtz)

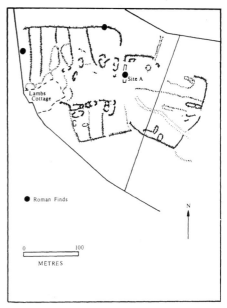

continued occupation of the small town by its Romano-British population. At Stonea (Cambridgeshire) excavations revealed clear evidence of the existence of a series of Anglo-Saxon buildings aligned on one of the original streets of the substantial Roman settlement.

Away from the areas affected by early Germanic migrations, there is strong evidence for site continuity after the end of the Roman period. At Camerton, for example, a cemetery lies adjacent to the prosperous industrial site, which was certainly thriving during the fourth century. The use of this cemetery appears to span a period from the late fourth century, through the pagan Saxon period and into the Christian early medieval period. This progression is suggested by the varied groupings of graves of different alignments and an association with different types of grave goods and burial rites.

In Somerset there is some evidence to suggest a fairly widespread movement of village settlements to local Iron Age hillforts, presumably as a result of instability in the countryside. At Cannington the Roman population appears to have shifted from the vulnerable port site of Combwich up into the Iron Age hillfort, where a very large sub-Roman cemetery remained in use into the medieval period.

The study of place-names can also be useful in any attempt at tracing possible continuity of Roman sites. The place-name *wicham*, for example, appears to be an Anglo-Saxon recognition of a continuing Romano-British settlement and is probably derived from the Latin *vicus*. The name Wycomb (Gloucestershire) is an example of this place-name, and at the site of Braughing (Hertfordshire) there is an associated *wicham* field-name.

11
Villages in other provinces

If the physical evidence provided by archaeology is to be placed in an historical context, the lack of historical sources relating to village communities in Roman Britain necessitates an examination of the evidence from other provinces. A comparison with other provinces will help our understanding of the nature and significance of village settlements and the everyday lives of their inhabitants. Unfortunately, what applies in one province may not necessarily do so in another. Caution is therefore necessary.

Gaul

The province with which Britain may be most usefully compared is Gaul (modern France). The two had many cultural similarities, although Gaul was Romanised to a far greater degree because of the longevity of the Roman occupation. In Gaul the tribal areas (*civitates peregrinae*) were divided up into units approximating parishes (*pagi*). Each *pagus* is thought to have had a large village (*vicus*) at its centre and most inscriptions relating to *vici* are found on major roads. In terms of access to justice, it has been noted that the Gallic Helvetti tribe looked to the local *vicus* for the resolution of minor matters but to the magistrate resident in the nearest *civitas* capital town for more serious cases.

With regard to a possible role for these settlements in local administration, a key body would have been the village council (*ordo*), the presence of which is indicated in a number of Gallic *vici*. Similar bodies administered the major towns and in Roman Britain the *ordo* of a *civitas* capital is recorded in an inscription from Caerwent in South Wales. Not every village would necessarily have sustained an *ordo*, however, as this body probably had a specific purpose in the administration of local government. Councils would have been found only within the largest rural settlements and in this context it is interesting to note that the fourth-century Theodosian code refers to the existence of 'mother villages' (*metrocomiae*).

Other similarities may be drawn with sites in Roman Gaul. The settlement at Arlon may usefully be compared with that at Bourton discussed in chapter 9. In both cases the Iron Age population appears to have relocated from an Iron Age centre towards a new Roman road.

The Gallic *vici* are also seen as important centres of production and distribution, each serving as a focus for villa settlement as in Britain. This economic significance is supported by inscriptions such as that from the village of Le Heraple, which indicates the presence of a local

47. The *conciliabulum* at Ribemont-sur-Ancre, France. Note the large temple complex and associated theatre. Compare with the plan of Wycomb, Gloucestershire, figure 35. (After Drinkwater)

merchant (*negotiator*). Some of the larger sites in Gaul appear to have functioned as centres for religious activity (*conciliabula*), as noted in chapter 9 (figure 47).

Many Gallic sites were fortified in the later Roman period, acting as strong points on the main roads. One difference between the *vici* of Gaul and the small towns of Britain is in their size. Some Gallic sites are very large and of semi-urban status and appearance, with sites like Arlon extending over some 60 acres (25 ha) (although in Britain sites such as Water Newton almost certainly had some form of official urban status by the later Roman period). In this context it is interesting to note that many *vici* in the Eastern Empire were elevated to municipal status in order to increase the number of *curiales*.

It seems likely, based on the evidence from Gaul, that a number of the small towns of Britain would have been termed *vici* during the Roman period although the use of that word is fraught with difficulties. However, it is probable that by the fourth century the term had degenerated into meaning a village of any type.

Other provinces

It is clear that in many parts of the empire village communities were directly owned by absentee landlords who employed the services of a local bailiff (*vilicus*). In Egypt lands farmed by tenants were termed *possessiones*. In some cases villages appear to have been named after their owner or patron, as in the case of the *Vicus Quintionis* in Thrace and the *Vicus Annaei* in north Africa.

In Asia Minor the majority of villages were directly owned by city dwellers or by the cities themselves, with village rental incomes no doubt helping to support the city *decurion* classes. In Syria contemporary sources identify villages as either freehold (*publici vici*) or owned (*possessiones*). In eastern provinces such as Thrace urban centres certainly appear to have owned vast territories encompassing a number of villages, the inhabitants of which paid taxes and rents to the towns. It is possible that a similar situation may have applied in Britain on a smaller scale. For example, the *colonia* of Gloucester had a number of villages in very close proximity which may well have been within the *territorium* of that town. It is likely that most *vici* in the empire came under the overall administrative control of the local *civitas* centre, but they nevertheless retained a degree of administrative authority.

Other settlement sites appear to have been owned by affluent temple complexes, as in the case of the Syrian temple to Doliche at Baitocaece. It is possible that small towns like Springhead (Kent) are British examples of temple ownership.

Further evidence relating to village administration is recorded in the province of Moesia, where inscriptions indicate the existence of the magistrates and *ordo* recorded in Gaul, as well as for another village officer, the tax assessor (*quinquennalis*). Minor officials recorded at the village of Katorkia in Asia Minor include two magistrates (*magistri*), elders (*gerousia*), a scribe (*grammatus*) and a market official (*agoronomos*). Another officer who appears in the sources is the local finance officer (*questor*).

The important marketing role played by the villages of the empire is indicated in many provinces. In Africa villages holding markets were given the official title of *nundinae* and at Skaptopara in Thrace the village inhabitants complained to the emperor about a large seasonal fair held close to their village. All the evidence suggests that the larger villages of the empire fulfilled a vital function as market centres.

To what extent historical evidence of this type can be applied to Roman Britain will never be certain, but what is clear is that the village form of settlement represents one of the most vital economic and administrative units within the empire. It is also likely that the majority of the empire's population lived within these types of rural communities. A study of village settlements, in which the inhabitants were essentially native in origin, provides an insight into the impact of Roman government on native populations.

12
Further reading

General surveys

Burnham, B.C. 'The Origins of Romano-British Small Towns', *Oxford Journal of Archaeology* 5 (1986).

Burnham, B.C. 'The Morphology of Romano-British Small Towns', *The Archaeological Journal* 144 (1987).

Burnham, B., and Wacher, J. *The Small Towns of Roman Britain.* Batsford, 1990. A useful summary of the evidence for each site.

Hingley, R. *Rural Settlement in Roman Britain.* Seaby, 1989. The best recent review of the evidence, incorporating plenty of new thinking.

Miles, D. (editor). *The Romano-British Countryside.* British Archaeological Reports 103, 1982.

Rodwell, W., and Rowley, T. (editors). *The Small Towns of Roman Britain.* British Archaeological Reports 15, 1975.

Site reports

Leech, R. *Excavations at Catsgore 1970–73.* Western Archaeological Trust, 1982.

Potter, T. 'The Roman Occupation of the Central Fenland', *Britannia* 12 (1981), pages 99–133.

Potter, T., and Jackson, R. (editors). *Excavations at Stonea, Cambridgeshire, 1980–85.* British Museum Press, 1996.

Rawes, B. 'The Romano-British Site at Brockworth, Gloucestershire', *Britannia* 12 (1981), pages 45–77.

Rawes, B. 'The Romano-British Site on the Portway', *Transactions of the Bristol and Gloucestershire Archaeological Society* (1984).

Wedlake, W.J. *Camerton.* Camerton Field Club, 1958.

Index

Page numbers in italic refer to illustrations